Printed in the United States of America
First Printing: June 2013
ISBN-978-0-989-4358-0-2

Some information and map data courtesy of United States
Geological Survey, U.S. National Park Service, Florida
Department of Parks and Recreation, Southwest Florida Water
Management District, Florida Department of Environmental
Protection, Florida Fish and Wildlife Commission, Sarasota
County Convention and Visitors Bureau, Grande Tours Kayak
and Paddle Board Center.

Paddles in Paradise

By

Edward and Deborah Higgins

Paddle on!

Deb Higgins

Ed Higgins

Frog Pond Publishing

2013

ACKNOWLEDGEMENTS

We'd like to thank all our friends and fellow paddlers at the Punta Gorda Boat Club. Without their encouragement this book would not have happened. Our group has grown so much this book is not long enough to thank all of you individually, but there are some in particular that we must single out:

We thank our friend, artist and fellow author, Howard Spielman and his wife, our dear friend, Shirley for your suggestions, support, help in editing, and most importantly the suggestion for the title of our book. It's perfect.

Thanks to Ron and Jan Norvelle who started the kayak group within the PGBC, convinced us to join, and then asked us to become the leaders. See what you started?

Thank you Bruce Weisgerber for your help in reviewing our first draft. By offering a set of new eyes and fresh guidance you helped make this book even more readable.

Frank and Sue Anne Fambrough and Lenora Weisgerber; you are always ready and willing to go exploring with us to find new places to paddle. We thank you.

We also must recognize all our friends who have shown up to help us when we gave kayak lessons: Frank Fambrough, James Fricke, Joe and Linda Guilivo, Rich and Pat Jacoby, Brenda Kramer, Tony & Teresa Manisco, Ron & Jan Norvelle, Shirley & Howard Spielman and Frank & Jan Walker. You gave your time, your kayaks and your expertise to help us teach new paddlers. We thank you all for helping us to introduce them to this wonderful world we share; these "Paddles in Paradise."

A special thank you also to Alex and Brenda Kramer. Whether it be helping the renters in and out of the water at Mount Dora, or staying back with the stragglers, you are always there to help and never fail to ask if you can do anything that will help to make someone's experience even better.

Lastly, but most especially, I want to personally thank Deb, my wife and best friend. Your countless hours of research for our paddles and this book are what made it all possible.

Your love, devotion, and companionship, through all of our adventures in life, are my rock and my *Raison d'être*....You are the words to my song.

INTRODUCTION

Deb and I retired and moved to Punta Gorda, Florida five years ago. It is a magical place where senior citizens become young again. The sun shines almost every day, flowers and wildlife are abundant, and retired folks with time on their hands are more active now than when they were young and working.

Our children and grandchildren think we are down here growing old. Boy, have we and our friends fooled them.

Sailing and power boating are everyday events, 70 year old bicyclists ride 20 miles just to warm up, the gyms are full of senior citizens, golf courses are busy and relatively inexpensive, and buying a kayak seems to be high on everyone's bucket list.

We are the leaders of a kayaking group within the boat club we belong to and along with "I've always wanted to try kayaking," the most often heard statement is "I wouldn't have any idea where to go." So we teach them; and we take them; and the response we get is amazing.

So we are reaching out even further. To those of you who love canoeing or kayaking, as well as those who want to try it, and don't know where to go in this area, this Bud's for you. Uh, book, I meant book.

The paddles listed in this book are paddles that you can easily do if you are a novice to an intermediate paddler. How do we find them? Some are really obvious and well known. We read books. We search the internet blogs. We talk to outfitters and other paddlers whenever we can, but most of all, we go exploring. When we find a place that seems interesting we go out and paddle it ourselves before we ever take anyone else. We have done every paddle in this book, most of them many times and we guarantee that the beauty of these paddles, and the nature around you, will keep you going back for more.

A quick word about kayaks and canoes. People are constantly asking us what kind of kayak or canoe they should buy. There is no answer we can give that works for everyone and this book is about *where* to paddle, not *what* you should invest your hard earned money in. Like people, canoes and kayaks are all different. No one kayak or canoe is any better or worse than another. It comes down to personal preference. Some like sit on tops; some like sit ins; some want a tandem; some want heavy duty strong and some want ultra light. You need to try out various makes and models. Get in or on one and paddle. Then try a different kind and paddle some more. You will eventually find the one that feels most comfortable and natural for *you*.

Having said that, there are several observations we can make from experience:

First, find one with a really good seat with back support, preferably one that you can adjust. After several hours in a paddle craft you will be *very* thankful for a good seating system.

Second, buy the best paddle you can afford. Paddles come in all shapes and sizes and just like your choice of kayak or canoe you should try out more than one. It may not seem like there is a very big difference physically between a $50 paddle and a $500 paddle but if you paddle a lot you'll know. The lighter the paddle the less fatigued you will get. Obviously, as recreational paddlers, we aren't advocating running out and buying a $500 paddle but a $200 paddle is well worth the expense if you can afford it. But, if you can only afford a used Craigslist paddle do not let that stop you from paddling your heart out. You will be in the same water, see the same sights and hear the same sounds as everyone else, even if you are a little more tired at the end of the day.

Lastly, the length of your kayak or canoe should be considered. There are many sizes of kayaks and canoes for a variety of purposes. Whitewater is different from recreation. Recreation is different from touring. Touring is different from ocean racing, etc. This book is all about recreational paddling. For what we do, and where we go, we have found that 12 to 14 feet is optimum. Any longer than that, and some of the tighter and narrower places may be more difficult to maneuver, any shorter and you will have a little more work to keep up with other paddlers. Again, having said that, the kayaks and canoes in our group are made up of a wide variety of types, sizes, and paddles so whatever your choice, go for it. *Recreation* is the operative word and believe me we are really, *really* good at recreating!

Oh, and one more thing. We may mention alligators in some of our descriptions. Relax! Alligators are a natural part of Florida wildlife. Anywhere there is fresh water in Florida you may see alligators. Don't worry. Alligators are more wary of you than you are of them. They are nocturnal feeders and humans are not on their diet. If you see an alligator during the day he or she is probably sleeping on a bank or lazily floating in the river. They will either ignore you completely or submerge under the water to hide. The number one rule of paddling in waters that contain alligators is, "ignore them and they will ignore you," also interpreted as "don't even think about feeding or touching the gator." We have paddled numerous times with alligators without any incidents whatsoever. If you practice "live and let live" with alligators you most assuredly ~~will~~ ~~definitely~~ ~~certainly~~ ~~usually~~ *may* live!

First disclaimer: This book is certainly not meant to totally encompass all the places you can canoe or kayak in Southwest Florida. There are literally thousands of great and accessible waters in our area. We have paddled many but we certainly haven't paddled them all, so we have pared our list to some of our favorites based on several criteria that we use within our kayak group:

✦ In this book we limit our excursions to relatively tame waters; waters that are perfect for beginner to intermediate paddlers. Although many of our paddlers are younger, quite accomplished, and strong, we also have many seniors as well as novice paddlers hoping to enjoy the sport as well; so we try to accommodate the group as a whole. When possible we try to avoid windy open water or strong currents. Thus, the paddles we include are recreational and not "exercise" paddles.

✦ Although Deb and I have done some really great paddles that are remote and entail launching in more difficult places, we have tried to limit this book to paddles that have easier launch sites and plenty of parking. With a group that sometimes reaches 40 or more paddlers on any given day, conveniences such as parking, ease of launch, picnic space and, of course, bathroom facilities become very important. Therefore the paddles listed in this book, for the most part, meet these criteria.

✦ We also have more than a few paddlers in our group who do not own their own kayaks or canoes and want rentals. Where possible if an outfitter is available we will include that information as well, although information that is valid today may not be valid six months or a year from now. Doing your own homework on rental availability at any of these paddles is advised.

✦ Finally, we are *recreational* paddlers. We have time on our hands. We have no deadlines. We have no interest in getting anywhere fast. We don't want to see big go-fast boats, housing developments or high rise buildings. We really enjoy the experience of being out in nature in places, some of which, you will never see unless you are in a kayak or canoe.

The feeling we get when we are in a small creek with overhanging live oak trees covered in Spanish moss while watching great blue herons quietly stalking prey; or silently gliding past alligators on the banks and listening to wild owls call to each other; or spying a baby hawk on the branch in front of us, is a holy experience. When we are out in these places the outside world disappears. Time slows down. The sounds, the smells, the silence and the beauty are breathtaking. We are kids again. Everything is new and exciting. We are no longer jaded by all of our life and work experiences. We are seeing everything with new eyes, with new wonder.

If you have never had nature take your breath away, and even if you have, try some (or all) of these paddles and you will know exactly what we mean. Each paddle brings you a different sense of awe; a different interpretation of beauty; and a different awareness of what it means to be at peace.

Paddle on,

Ed & Deb

"Come to the edge,' He said. They said, 'We are afraid.'

'Come to the edge,' He said. They came.

He pushed them….and they flew."

….Guillaume Apollinaire

DEDICATION

This book is dedicated to those daring and adventurous souls who have allowed us to lead them into strange waters; trusting us completely when we told them that they could easily do this and that they would be in awe at the beauty around them.

They believed us….and they did…..and they were.

Table of Contents

The paddles in this book are not listed in any particular ranking but by alphabetical order

For those of you who would like to quickly find paddles in a particular area the paddles are listed alphabetically by County here:

Chapter 1

Braden River at Linger Lodge

GPS address   7205 85th Ct. East   Bradenton

Bashful baby alligator

The Braden River between Linger Lodge and Jiggs Landing is very scenic and sparsely developed. Wildflowers, birds and alligators can be seen.

This is a beautiful paddle along the river and it is doubly exciting if you have lunch at the Linger Lodge restaurant (http://www.lingerlodgeresort.com).

There is no launch fee but if you launch here it is good etiquette to have lunch at the lodge. You will not mind though, because it is a truly funky old and odd place. It has been quoted to be one of the top five weirdest restaurants in the country and the food is pretty good too. It's a great place to try frog's legs and gator bites as well as more mundane fare.

When you put in, head to the right out of the side canal and then turn to the right when you reach the main river.

It is about a 1.5 hour paddle between the lodge and Jiggs Landing where there is a parking and picnic area, a state-of-the art kayak launch, and restroom facilities.

Linger Lodge landing

Another leisurely day trip would be a launch at Jiggs Landing, (see Chapter 8) paddle to Linger Lodge, stop for lunch at the Lodge restaurant and return to Jiggs Landing.

From either end this is a two way paddle (up and back), but there are several bends and turns with tributaries in the river, so pay attention to your landmarks. Even if you take a wrong turn you'll just dead end and should easily find your way to the main river.

Rentals are available here but they don't have very many kayaks so call ahead if you plan on going and need a rental. Their phone # is 941-755-2757.

Directions to Braden River at Linger Lodge

Take I-75 North to exit 217B. Drive west on SR 70 for approximately 2 miles. Turn left onto Caruso Road. Caruso Road intersects with Braden River Road. Follow Braden River Road, bearing right, until you intersect with Linger Lodge Road. Turn left onto Linger Lodge Road and follow to the end. Turn right onto 85th Ct. East to the entrance of the campground. The boat ramp is to the left behind the restaurant. Allow approximately 1 hour from Punta Gorda.

Braden River…..Linger Lodge / Jiggs Landing

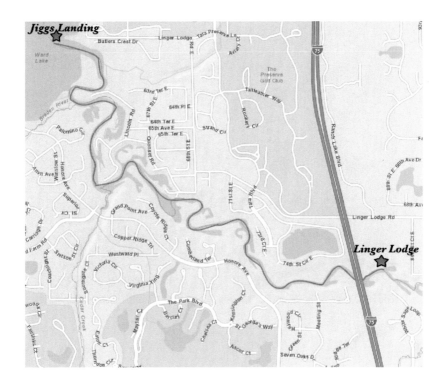

Chapter 2

Commodore Creek Trail

GPS address   900 Tarpon Bay Rd   Sanibel Island

White ibis

Commodore Creek Trail is a 2.5 mile marked and numbered trail in and out of the mangroves and is a very easy and scenic paddle.

After you launch turn to the left and cross a shallow bay. Look for the large blue sign marking the entrance and just follow the markers (numbered 1-17) through the mangroves and mud flats while watching for wading birds and marine wildlife. This is shallow tidal water so the time to go is on a rising or high tide in order to get completely through the trail.

If you want to make the paddle a little longer (about 20 minutes each way), either before or after heading to the trail, head straight out from the launch and paddle across the open bay to the bird rookery on the islands in front of you. You will see large numbers of anhinga, pelicans, and herons nesting there.

Entrance to Commodore Creek Trail

When you get to the Tarpon Bay Explorer's facility you can unload by the boat ramp and then park in the parking area. Upstairs at the store you can pay the launch fee ($7 per canoe/ kayak) or rent one for $25 for 2 hours and $12.50 each additional hour. There are restroom facilities and parking is free. There are also several picnic tables if you want to eat after your paddle.

6

Some of the outfitter's staff at the facility are not very accommodating if you bring your own canoe/kayak. They launch their rentals from a sandy beach but won't let you use that beach if you bring your own. You must use the concrete boat ramp, which is very slippery (even though you pay a pretty steep launch fee).

All in all, we like this paddle but we haven't always liked our experience with some of the personnel there. If you go you can tell them we said so. They just don't get it! We are *really* easy to get along with.

For tide and rental info you can contact them at www.tarponbayexplorers.com.

Directions to Tarpon Bay Explorers

Take I-75 South to exit 131. Drive west on Daniels Pkwy to the Ben Pratt/Six Mile Cypress intersection. At the stop light turn left onto Six Mile Cypress. At the next major light you will cross U.S. 41 and Six Mile Cypress changes its name to Gladiolus. Continue on Gladiolus, and turn left onto Summerlin Road. After driving over the Sanibel Causeway ($6 toll) turn right at the first stop sign onto Periwinkle Way. Follow about 3 miles to the 4 way stop and turn right onto Tarpon Bay Road. The Tarpon Bay Explorers facility is through the gates at the end of the road. Allow approximately 1 hour from Punta Gorda.

Commodore Creek Trail

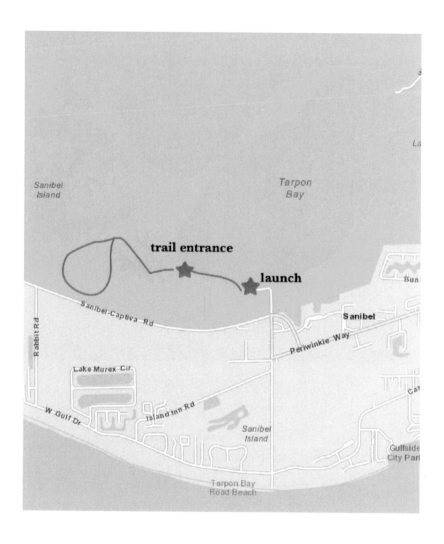

Chapter 3

Deer Prairie Creek

GPS address   10201 South Tamiami Trail   North Port

Landscape Florida style

Deer Prairie Creek is a really beautiful, scenic preserve especially suited to paddlers who want to go back in time.

This paddle is among our favorites. It is pristine, quiet and shaded with loads of "Old Florida" charm. You and the creek will meander through bends and turns at such a leisurely pace that you'll think time has stood still.

9

It will be less than 3 to 4 miles before you run out of water or reach impassable areas, but it is such a great paddle you will do it again and again.

You put in through the gate at the left corner of the parking lot just above the dam into a small lake. If you put in at the canoe/kayak launch you will be below the dam, and that is another paddle for another day.

This is an up and back paddle and it is impossible to get lost. Just head to your right after launch and expect to see luscious flora, wildflowers, birds and possibly a gator or two.

The biggest downside here is that there is only a port-a-potty for a bathroom facility and it is not always serviced very well.

Deb at Deer Prairie Creek

There are several picnic tables you can use for lunch, and while there are no on-site rentals, we use a really great outfitter out of Punta Gorda who will service you there for a small delivery charge in addition to the rental fee. Call Vince at O-SEA-D Aquatic Adventures in Punta Gorda. This outfitter is very accommodating and provides it all; kayak sales and rentals, guided trips, eco tours, moonlight paddles, you name it….he will accommodate you. They are also some of the friendliest folks we have met.

You can find them at:

http://www.oseadkayaking.com. phone 941-347-8102

Directions to Deer Prairie Creek Preserve

Take Rte 41 North (Tamiami Trail) into North Port. You will pass "Warm Mineral Springs" on your right. From the Warm Mineral Springs sign proceed 1.5 miles and look for a white shell unpaved road.

The entrance sign cannot be seen directly from the road but once you turn onto it the sign is visible set back by the entrance gate. Follow the road all the way to the end to the parking lot.

Do NOT stop at the "canoe/kayak launch" sign but drive to the parking area at the end of the road. Allow approximately 30 minutes from Punta Gorda.

Deer Prairie Creek

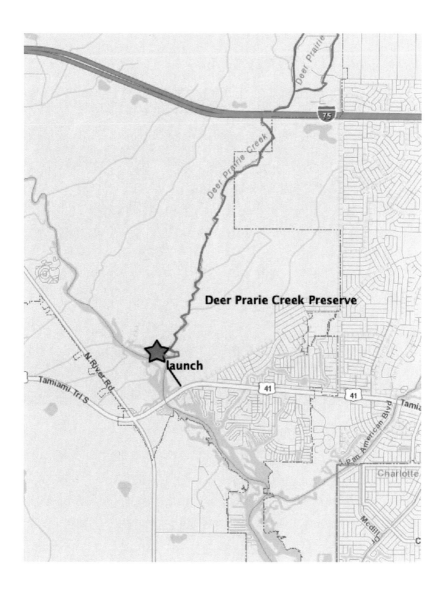

Chapter 4

Dora Canal

GPS address   1001 Wells Ave   Tavares

Red-shouldered hawk

The Dora Canal is only a one mile canal linking Lake Dora and Lake Eustis but may be one of the most beautiful miles you'll ever experience. This is a short paddle so do it very slowly. Wildlife is abundant if you take the time to look. On our last trip we saw alligators, herons, red-shouldered hawks, brown water snakes, egrets, and an amazing array of "Old Florida" flora, including some giant cypress trees that are reported to be 2000 years old.

Take the time to experience the beauty of the Dora Canal. When you reach Lake Eustis turn around and slowly paddle back, absorbing the grandeur of mother nature.

Some of the filming for the movie "African Queen" was shot here and it's easy to see why.

Since this is such a short paddle consider this for the first afternoon of a multi-day trip. Drive up to Mt Dora and check in at your hotel (we prefer the Lakeside Inn); paddle the Dora Canal then go back to your hotel for a swim and cocktails by the pool before dinner out in downtown Mt Dora.

We are, after all, *recreational* paddlers!

Anhinga at Dora Canal

Second Disclaimer: At certain times there can be a lot of boat traffic in the canal which can take away from the overall experience. Ignore it as best you can, concentrate on the beauty around you, and before you know it you'll forget they are there.

Although Mt Dora is a 3 hour drive from Punta Gorda, there are several great paddles in this area (see Wekiva River Ch 24, Silver River Ch 18, and Rock Springs Run Ch 16). It is well worth an overnight stay to do multiple paddles while you are there.

This is one of our group's favorite overnight trips and we regularly have 40-50 people attend when we do it.

Directions to Summerall Park

Take I-75 North to exit 261 and follow I-4 East until exit 38 (Florida 33 North) Follow 33 North approximately 33 miles and turn left onto E Broad St/Orange St. Turn right onto Florida 19 North. Follow 19 North approximately 19 miles and turn right onto Wells Ave. Take 2nd right onto Rose Ave. Summerall Park is on the corner of Wells and Rose Aves. Allow approximately 3 hours from Punta Gorda.

When you get to Summerall Park in Tavares do not take the main park entrance on Wells Ave but go to the corner of Rose Ave and drive into the rear parking area (closest to the boat ramp). You can unload there and park nearby as well. Paddle out of the short canal, turn left into the main canal, and you will go back in time.

Dora Canal

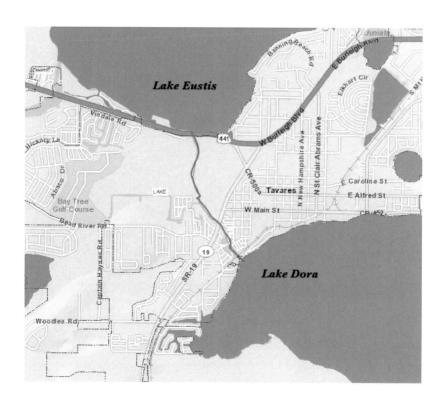

Chapter 5

Fisheating Creek

GPS address   7555 U.S. 27   Palmdale

A spiritual place

This has to be one of the most beautiful paddles anywhere and it is our personal favorite. As I have said many times about many a river we were on: "this is where I go to church." Well, Fisheating Creek is our St Peter's Basilica.

Fisheating Creek is a black water cypress swamp and paddling here makes you realize why you do this. The natural beauty of this place is breathtaking. Don't be surprised if you become speechless at the magnificence of it all. It is that overwhelming. At least it is to us. Obviously, a cypress swamp may not be everyone's taste but it certainly is ours.

After launching, head straight upriver (not left) and expect to see all types of Florida birds, beautiful old cypress trees, live oaks with hanging Spanish moss, wildflowers and maybe an alligator or two. If you keep your eyes peeled you could even see deer, turkey and wild pigs.

The time of year you do this paddle is important because the water levels fluctuate with the rains. If the water is too low you will not get very far without having to portage, and if the water is too high you will have a hard time finding your way through the maze of cypress. The Outpost website states that you need a minimum level of 2 feet for a canoe, however we have kayaked there with 3 feet and had to make several portages. We have found that 4-5 feet was optimum.

Cypress trees along Fisheating Creek

Directions to Fisheating Creek Outpost

From I-75 exit 164 take 17 East to Bermont Road. Turn right on Bermont Road (SR 74) and drive 42 miles. At end turn left onto Rte 29. At intersection of Rte 27 and 29 turn left onto Rte 27. Entrance to Fisheating Creek Outpost/Campground is approximately 1.5 miles on your left over the railroad tracks. Allow approximately 1 hour from Punta Gorda.

You will stop at the Outpost store as you enter the campground and pay a $2 parking/launch fee per canoe/kayak before heading over to the launch area.

After unloading, park in the main parking area which is only a short walk from the launch. The Outpost has rentals available, restrooms, a picnic area, and even provides guided paddle trips if you're so inclined. They are very friendly and usually will help you with your gear and launching.

They also have a website that posts the water level daily. The Outpost will also shuttle you up for an 8 mile one way trip. You can find them at:

http://www.fisheatingcreekoutpost.com.

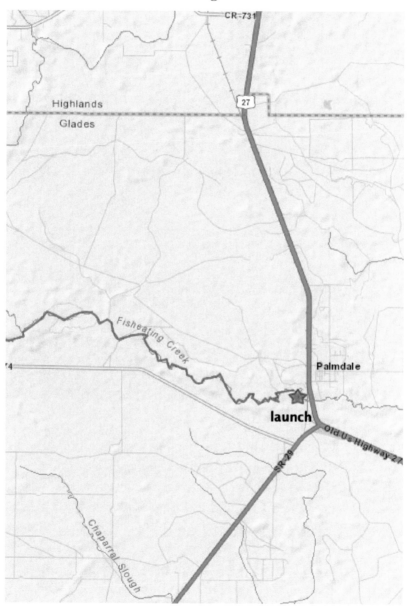

Chapter 6

Hells Bay Trail

GPS address   40001 State Road 9336   Homestead

Deep in the Everglades

This is a long, and mostly sheltered, paddle weaving through small ponds and mangroves along creeks dotted with small islands, and opening into several small bays. You will see beautiful bromeliads throughout the trail which has dark stained water from the red mangrove trees. The high arching roots of the trees create shelter and protection for fish and crabs. An occasional alligator might be seen along clearings on the banks. You will be tired but proud that you negotiated your way through the wilderness and back to your car.

There is a marked and numbered trail that will take you 11 miles round trip if you follow it to the Hell's Bay Chickee but you can opt to turn around at the Pearl Bay Chickee (3.5 miles) or at Lard Can Campsite (3 miles). Make sure to follow the markers; sometimes they only come into view just about the time you think you missed one. Look closely; the mangroves have grown over some of them but they are there.

This is truly paddling in the Everglades and is not a place where you want to get lost.

Ed at Lard Can on Hell's Bay Trail

After the paddle, in honor of Ben Franklin (see page 47) hydrate....re-hydrate...and celebrate....that you live, and/or paddled, in paradise.

When you do this paddle it will be an overnight in Homestead or Florida City and you can do Nine Mile Pond Trail (see Ch 12) and Noble Hammock Trail (see Ch 13) on the same trip. The best time to do these Everglade trips is in the fall or winter….You won't have enough bug spray with you for a summer paddle!

Directions to Everglades Visitor Center

Take I-75 South across Alligator Alley. Take Exit 5 for Florida's Turnpike South towards Key West. Merge onto Florida 821 South. Drive approximately 38 miles and exit left onto US 1 S / NE 1st Ave toward Key West. Turn right onto SW 344th St / E Palm Drive. Stay on this road for about 1 1/2 miles then turn left onto Tower Road. Drive 2 miles then turn right onto State Road 9336 until you reach the Ernest Coe Visitor Center Gate in Everglades National Park. Allow approximately 3 ¼ hours from Punta Gorda.

There are no facilities at the parking/launch area but there are at the West Lake area several miles further towards Flamingo. Rentals were available when we were there (http://www.toursintheeverglades.com) but we recommend calling ahead. The National Park Service has several paddle trail maps on-line with great information on the trails at http://www.nps.gov/ever/planyourvisit/canoe-and-kayak-trails.htm. Print them out and bring them with you.

There is a $10 entrance fee to the Park which is good for 7 days (if you are over 62 and have a National Parks Senior Pass it is free) and a $1.50 launch fee per canoe/kayak. From the Everglades Park entrance it is a long 30+ mile drive along the main park road to Nine Mile Pond trail. Hell's Bay trail is just a few miles further along the same road, shortly beyond Noble Hammock Trail. You will see the sign for the trail and you can park and launch right on the side of the road.

Hell's Bay Trail

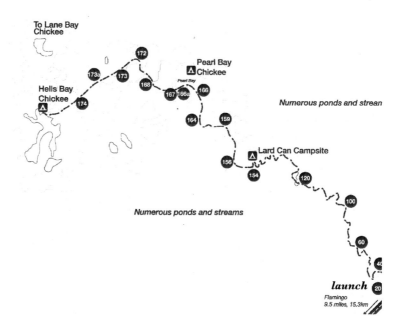

Chapter 7

Imperial River

GPS address   10375 Pennsylvania Ave   Bonita Springs

The scenic Imperial River

Eureka! We have found a hidden gem smack dab in the middle of civilization. The Imperial River, from Riverside Park up to the I-75 bridge, is as scenic as you can get considering there is development along most of the length. Although there are homes along the river, they are set back away from the banks and they never intrude into the serene beauty of this paddle.

Your feeling of isolation is complete as you paddle along this river and pass beneath the overhanging canopy of live oak while noting the wild bamboo soaring sixty feet in the air.

During this trip you will see an amazing variety of plants, trees, and flowers. Palm, pine, cypress, bamboo, royal poinciana, wild tamarind, and sweetbay magnolia are abundant and untouched.

In the spring, you can expect to see and smell many blooming wildflowers, including wild azalea, St John's wort, buttonbush, periwinkle and wild mint. It is also not uncommon to see alligators and manatees as you leisurely paddle along.

When you do this paddle you will feel as if time has stood still. With its rustic "Old Florida" charm you will not notice the civilization all around you but will bask in the beauty and peace of this river.

Do it once, and you'll do it again….and again….and again!

Wild…...yet tame

Driving Directions to Riverside Park

Take I-75 South to Exit 116 Bonita Springs. Merge right onto Bonita Beach Road. Drive approximately 1.7 miles and turn right onto Old 41 Road. Drive approximately 1/2 mile and turn left onto Pennsylvania Ave. Cross the railroad tracks and on your right will be a parking lot for Riverside Park. Enter parking lot and drive to the back of the lot to a dirt road. Take the dirt road down to the launch area beside the railroad bridge. Allow approximately 1 hour from Punta Gorda.

This launch area is behind the main park, just across the railroad tracks. You can unload your gear right by the wooden pedestrian bridge and either park right there (leaving the road accessible), or park back up in the paved parking area, a short walk away, near the restroom facility.

You will launch to the right of the bridge and head to the right on the river. You can paddle as far as the I-75 bridge before you run out of water; a distance of about 2.5 miles that will take less than 3 hours round trip.

The park has picnic areas, restrooms, and free parking.

For rentals there is an outfitter on site in the main park area on the street side of the railroad tracks. They are located in the last artist cottage closest to the river and are very friendly and accommodating. You can reach them at:

http://www.calusaghosttours.com.

Imperial River

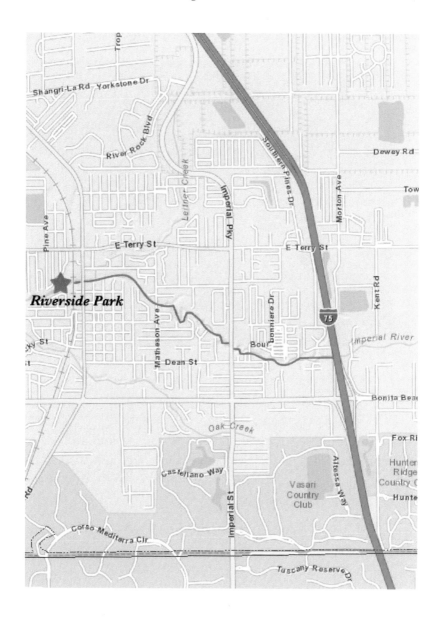

Chapter 8

Jiggs Landing

GPS address   6106 63rd St East   Bradenton

Kayak launch at Jiggs Landing

This paddle begins at a state-of-the-art canoe/kayak launch which has a roller system that allows you to get into and out of the water completely dry. You simply put your canoe/kayak on the dock, get in, and pull yourself along the handrails into the water. Getting out is just as easy.

You'll paddle straight across a small open lake heading slightly to the left. You will see the entrance marked by a channel sign. You are now in the Braden River heading towards Linger Lodge. This is the same paddle as the Braden River Paddle (see Ch 1) except going in the opposite direction.

If you depart from Jiggs Landing it is about a 1.5 hour leisurely paddle to Linger Lodge where you'll want to stop, stretch, and have lunch at one of Florida's funkiest restaurants before paddling back to the landing.

Braden River Flora

If you don't want to paddle all the way to the Lodge, head out for an hour or so, turn around and head back.

There are some twists and turns along the river so pay attention to your landmarks.

Directions to Jiggs Landing Preserve

Take I-75 North to exit 217B. Drive west on SR 70. Turn left onto Caruso Road. Caruso Road intersects with 63rd St east (also know and labeled as Braden River Road). Follow to the end, and at the intersection of Linger Lodge Road, Jiggs Landing Preserve will be on your right. Allow approximately 1 hour drive time from Punta Gorda.

Jiggs Landing has plenty of free parking and has great facilities for picnicking, as well as restrooms, but has no outfitter on-site for rentals. However, there is an outfitter in the area who does guided trips on the River. You can try them at:

http://www.thecanoeoutpost.com.

Braden River…..Linger Lodge / Jiggs Landing

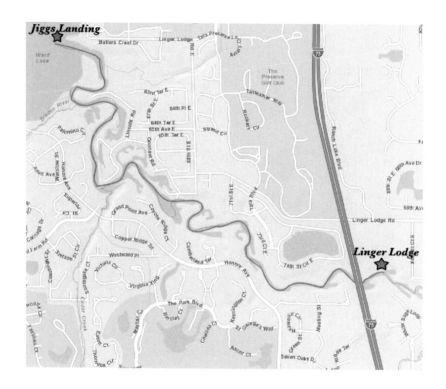

Chapter 9

Lido Key Mangrove Trail

GPS address   *190 Taft Drive*   *Sarasota*

Mangrove trail at Lido Key

This is an easy two hour paddle among the mangroves and protected waterways of Sarasota Bay. When you leave the launch head to the right. There are several trails in and out of the mangrove trees with abundant bird life. Dolphin and manatee sightings are common. This paddle offers the best of both worlds; some covered mangrove trails and some pretty Sarasota Bay open water. Like Turtle Beach, this is a great hot weather paddle. There is a nice sandbar along the route where you can get out of your canoe/kayak and stretch your legs, wade in the water, or enjoy a swim; so wear something you can get wet.

The park has a launch area as well as picnic and restroom facilities.

When you go be sure to avoid school vacation week. We know this because *we* went during school vacation week and the launch area and waterway was extremely crowded.

There are only a few picnic tables right at the launch area so on a busy day Plan B would be to go into St Armand's Circle and have lunch at one of the many restaurants there.

Watch out for hitchhikers along the way.

Rentals are available here but are expensive. The outfitters in this area will only do full day rentals, even if you are only going for a few hours. You can reach them at:

http://www.adventurekayakoutfitters.com or phone 941-779-7426

Directions to South Lido Beach Nature Park

Take I-75 North and take exit 210. Turn left off exit onto SR 780 West (Fruitville Road). Stay on Fruitville Road until intersection of US 41. Turn left onto US 41 South. Turn right onto Gulf Stream/John Ringling Causeway. As you enter St Armands Circle take the 2nd exit and continue on John Ringling Blvd. Follow to the end and bear left on Ben Franklin Drive. Follow to the intersection of Taft Drive. and turn left on Taft. The Park is directly in front of you. Allow approximately 1 hour from Punta Gorda.

Lido Key Mangrove Trail

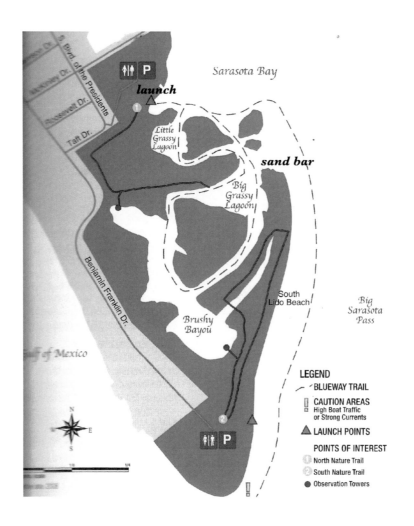

Chapter 10

Manatee Park

GPS address   10901 Palm Beach Blvd   Ft Myers

Curious manatees at Manatee Park

This paddle is a favorite in the winter months (November-March) because the manatees migrate into the warm discharge waters of the power plant and pretty much just hang out until their natural waters warm up again.

There are, actually, 2 nice paddles from this particular park. In January and February turn right and plan on just barely paddling around while enjoying seeing manatees up close and personal right outside the power plant discharge. From the launch area paddle through a short narrow waterway until you come out into open water and turn right. You can continue paddling in that direction and you will be headed towards the Caloosahatchee River. You will see manatees all along the way and, by far, the best way to experience manatees is from your kayak/canoe.

Alligators are also not an uncommon sight along the banks. This is a more developed section of water so you will also see more civilization and hear more traffic.

If you turn left when exiting the launch area you will be paddling up the Orange River (see Ch 14). This is a much more scenic paddle but you'll probably see fewer manatees. Birds, turtles and fish will be abundant as well as an alligator or two. It is a two way paddle (up and back) so you can paddle however long you wish.

Sleeping alligator on the Orange River

When we go to Manatee Park after the manatees have left we always head up the Orange River for a very peaceful and relaxed paddle.

Directions to Manatee Park

Take I-75 South to exit 141 (just over the Caloosahatchee bridge) and take a left off the exit. Drive east for 1.25 miles. Manatee Park is on the right directly across the street from the FPL power plant. Allow approximately 30 minutes from Punta Gorda.

When you drive in follow the signs to the kayak/canoe launch area and unload your gear before moving your vehicle to the parking area. There is a parking fee of $1 per hour with a maximum $5. Don't forget to get a fee envelope from the self pay station and leave the stub on your dashboard. There is plenty of parking although during the high season it can get crowded with non paddlers.

The park has restrooms, a store, picnic areas, kayak and canoe rentals from the store, and a paved walkway and viewing area to see the manatees from shore.

If it's manatees you came to see it's not a bad idea to check the rental company's website first which will give you the manatee count at the park. As the water begins to warm up it's not unusual for them to disappear overnight.

http://www.calusabluewayoutfitters.com.

http://www.leeparks.org.

Manatee Park / Orange River

Chapter 11

Myakka River State Park

GPS address   13208 SR 72   *Sarasota*

A few of the local denizens

This is THE paddle if you want to see alligators. If you do not want to see alligators this is NOT the paddle for you.

The allure of this paddle is the wildlife, especially the alligators. It is an up and back trip so paddle as long as you like while remembering that you have to paddle back. Bring your camera so you can show all the city folk that, yes, you were actually in the water with alligators and survived; (just don't swim there though…..you want to keep the camera dry).

We have done this paddle many times and have seen, literally, hundreds of alligators on the banks and in the water with never an incident. Remember in the introduction (I hope you read it) the first rule of paddling with alligators? Here it is again: "ignore them and they will ignore you," which is also interpreted as "don't even think about feeding or touching the gator."

Relax and enjoy seeing the alligators. They enjoy seeing you....Yum....hmmm.

This is a downstream paddle through grasslands and some neat wooded areas. Although this paddle is certainly not a difficult one, it could sometimes be rated as moderate if it is windy while paddling back upstream. It is not a strong current but it is a current.

Gator heaven on the Myakka River

When you are done paddling, the park is a great place to explore. There are trails, a must-see canopy walkway and tower, as well as a store, restaurant, restrooms and canoe/kayak rentals.

Directions to Myakka River State Park

Take I-75 North to exit 170 (King's Hwy). Turn right and take King's Hwy east until the intersection of SR 72. Turn left onto SR 72 and go approximately 25 miles. The Park entrance will be on your right. Proceed into the park along the entrance road (it's a long road) to the furthest parking lot, past the concessions. Allow approximately 1 hour from Punta Gorda

The park is open at 8am until sunset and there is a $6 entry fee per vehicle.

Unload your gear at the launch in the right rear of the parking lot, at the end of the airboat canal, then park your vehicle in the lot. You will launch here and paddle around the left shore line to the observation post and the spillway/weir. (You can carry your canoe/kayak through the woods and launch at the weir but it is a trek). If the water is high you can paddle right on by but low water will require getting out and re-launching on the other side. This is not a weir with rapid flowing water, just an obstacle across the river.

Rentals are $20 for the first hour and $5 for each additional hour.

Most people stop at the bridge on the way in or out and watch the alligators down below.

For info on the park go to http://www.myakkariver.org.

Myakka River State Park

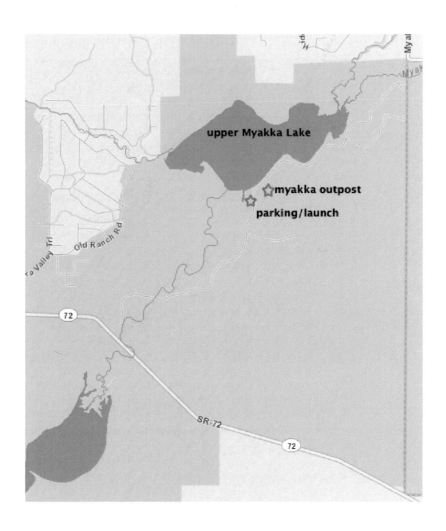

Chapter 12

Nine Mile Pond

GPS address   40001 State Rd 9336   Homestead

Alone in the wilderness

The trail at Nine Mile Pond is not 9 miles. It got its name because it was 9 miles from the Indian Store that was there at the time, so relax; you only have 5 miles to go.

The paddle is not difficult but it does take some stamina. This is a five mile loop through shallow grass flats and scattered mangrove swamps and will take 4-5 hours to complete at a leisurely pace. The varied wildlife and plant life along the way make it a worthwhile and stunning experience.

Along this trail expect to see the usual wading birds, alligators, turtles, fish, and at the end of the trail we even saw a *big* American Crocodile. Bromeliads and air plants are abundant among the mangroves and buttonwood trees. There are also bladderwort, a meat eating plant which has small yellow flowers and feeds on mosquito larvae. Speaking of mosquitos, this paddle is for the cooler months when the mosquito level is lower (notice I said lower, not *low*). Bring mosquito spray; you will need it. Also bring plenty of water and some snacks. After the paddle you can also go to the Flamingo visitors center and grab a sandwich if you didn't bring your own.

One of many mangrove tunnels at Nine Mile Pond

After crossing the open water of Nine Mile Pond you will get to the first of 116 white marker poles. There is a shortcut at marker # 44A which will shorten the paddle by about 1.5 miles. If you take the shortcut bear left at the "shortcut" marker and cut across the open marsh to marker #82. You need to paddle close to marker #82 before you can see marker #83. Many of the markers are spread out and may seem difficult to find but just stay cool, take your time and you will find them.

Remember, this is the Everglades. It is remote. It is pristine. It is *remote*. Just to be able to say you've paddled here makes you worthy of the title "Paddler in Paradise."

Ben Franklin said: "Beer is proof that God loves us and wants us to be happy." We say: "The Everglades are proof that God loves us and wants us to be happy." However, let's go with good old Ben on this one and don't forget to hydrate after the paddle.

Directions to Everglades Visitor Center

Take I-75 South across Alligator Alley. Take Exit 5 for Florida's Turnpike South towards Key West. Merge onto Florida 821 South. Drive approximately 38 miles and exit left onto US 1 S / NE 1st Ave toward Key West. Turn right onto SW 344th St / E Palm Drive. Stay on this road for about 1.5 miles then turn left onto Tower Road. Drive 2 miles then turn right onto State Road 9336 until you reach the Ernest Coe Visitor Center Gate in Everglades National Park. Allow approximately 3 1/4 hours from Punta Gorda.

There is a $10 entrance fee to the Park which is good for 7 days (if you are over 62 and have a National Parks Senior Pass it is free) and a $1.50 launch fee per canoe/kayak. From the Park entrance it is a long 30+ mile drive along the main park road to Nine Mile Pond Trail. You will see the sign for the trail and you can park and launch right at the pond. There are no facilities at the parking/launch area but there are at the West Lake area several miles further towards Flamingo.

Rentals were available when we were there but you should call ahead. The National Park Service has several paddle trail maps on-line with great information about the trails. Print them out and bring them with you.

Rental outfitter: http://www.toursintheeverglades.com

Park Service: http://www.nps.gov/ever/planyourvisit/canoe-and-kayak-trails.htm

When you do this paddle it will be an overnight at Homestead or Florida City and you can do Hell's Bay Trail (see Ch 6) and Noble Hammock Trail (see Ch 13) on the same trip.

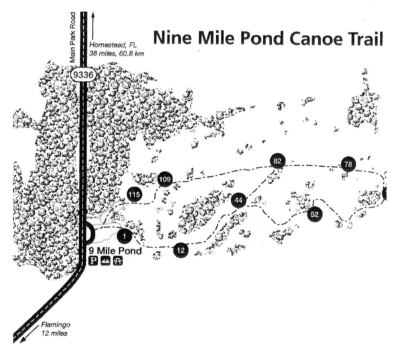

Chapter 13

Noble Hammock Trail

GPS address   40001 State Rd 9336   Homestead

Along Noble Hammock Trail

Noble Hammock trail is a 1.9 mile marked loop trail that winds through a veritable maze of mangrove trees as well as some small ponds as it circles Noble Hammock, reputedly a haven for moonshiners in the 1900's.

There are many sharp turns and very narrow passageways. If your canoe/kayak is longer than 16 feet you won't be able to negotiate the tight turns. You will most assuredly develop your paddle skills trying to maneuver through some of them. In fact, in some of the narrower passageways you will have to stow your paddle and pull yourself through hand over hand. Don't

49

let this discourage you. This is a particularly serene, remote trail and a true everglades paddle.

It will take at least 2 hours to complete since it is very slow going but it is a perfect paddle for windy days because it is so protected. You will probably scare up some lolling fish as you slip silently through the mangrove canopy, which in turn will probably startle you; but don't worry......the alligators keep the fish population in check!

Note: When you complete the loop on this trail you come out in a different location than where you put in. Don't panic when you get out of your canoe/kayak and your vehicle isn't there. Just look a few hundred yards to your right and it will be there, right where you left it. We suggest walking up and driving your vehicle back to your gear rather than toting it back.

Launch area at Noble Hammock Trail

Directions to Everglades Visitor Center

Take I-75 South across Alligator Alley. Take Exit 5 for Florida's Turnpike South towards Key West. Merge onto Florida 821 South. Drive approximately 38 miles and exit left onto US 1 S / NE 1st Ave toward Key West. Turn right onto SW 344th St / E Palm Drive. Stay on this road for about 1 1/2 miles then turn left onto Tower Road. Drive 2 miles then turn right onto State Road 9336 until you reach the Ernest Coe Visitor Center Gate in Everglades National Park. Allow approximately 3 ¼ hours from Punta Gorda.

There is a $10 entrance fee to the Park which is good for 7 days (if you are over 62 and have a National Parks Senior Pass it is free) and a $1.50 launch fee per canoe/kayak. From the Park entrance it is a long 30+ mile drive along the main park road to Noble Hammock Trail. You will see the sign for the trail and you can park and launch right at the trail on the left. There are facilities at the West Lake area several miles further towards Flamingo. Rentals were available when we were there (http://toursintheeverglades.com) but we recommend calling ahead. The National Park Service has several paddle trail maps on-line with great information about the trails at http://www.nps.gov/ever/planyourvisit/canoe-and-kayak-trails.htm. Print them out and bring them with you.

When you do this paddle it will be an overnight at a hotel in Homestead or Florida City (unless you live nearby...but not much is nearby) and you can do Hell's Bay Trail (see Ch 6) and Nine Mile Pond Trail see (Ch 12) on the same trip.

Chapter 14

Orange River

GPS address   10901 Palm Beach Blvd   Ft Myers

Air plants and Spanish moss dot the landscape

The Orange River is an up and back paddle so you can't get lost and you will thoroughly enjoy the scenery and peacefulness of the river.

This paddle has less development along the banks than if you went toward the Caloosahatchee and we have never run into very many paddlers along the way. It is fairly quiet for being so close to major roads and highways. It is a scenic paddle with plenty of wildlife, aquatic plants, flowers and, of course, the abundant Florida Live Oak and varied palm trees.

This is a great, close to home, relaxing paddle when you just want to get away for a few hours.

The starting point for this paddle is the same as the Manatee Park paddle (see Ch 10). Instead of heading to the right when you exit the launch area head to the left. You can easily do both the manatee sighting paddle and this one in a short day trip.

Alligator Lily along the Orange River

During the high (Winter) season the park can get pretty crowded with paddlers and non paddlers alike but most of them are there to see the manatees. If you head down the river you will soon find yourself in your happy place.

Directions to Manatee Park

Take I-75 South to exit 141 (just over the Caloosahatchee bridge) and take a left off the exit. Drive east for 1.25 miles. Manatee Park is on the right directly across the street from the FPL power plant. Allow approximately 30 minutes from Punta Gorda.

When you drive in follow the signs to the kayak/canoe launch area and unload your gear before moving your vehicle to the parking area. There is a parking fee of $1 per hour with a maximum $5. After you park you need to get a fee envelope from the self pay station and leave the stub on your dashboard. On busy weekend days there may be an attendant collecting the parking fee as you drive in. There will be plenty of parking available.

The park has restrooms, a store, picnic areas, and kayak and canoe rentals from the store. For information on the park and river go to:

http://www.leeparks.org/facility-info

Orange River

Chapter 15

Ponce de Leon Park

GPS address 3400 Ponce de Leon Parkway   Punta Gorda

Navigating the mangrove tunnels at Ponce Park

This is a short (less than 2 hours) leisurely paddle and needs to be done when the tide is rising or high. At low tide you will not be able to get through the tunnels.

The mangrove tunnels are fairly wide with mangrove trees forming a pretty, but not claustrophobic, canopy. Novice paddlers will easily be able to navigate them and you will see just what kind of remote beauty there is so close to the civilization all around you.

Ponce Park is on Charlotte Harbor at Ponce de Leon inlet. It is a small 10 acre park with a boardwalk through the wetlands, a wildlife sanctuary, boat ramp, picnic areas, sandy beach area and restroom facilities. This is all salt water, therefore, no alligators.

Unload your gear at the boat ramp and then park in the parking lot. Upon launching from the ramp turn left into the canal. Paddle a short distance and turn right into a small open water area. Paddle across the open water and look for the opening into the mangrove tunnel on far left. Follow the tunnel out into another open water area and turn right to the next opening. Follow this trail all the way through the tunnels.

As Yogi Berra said, "When you come to a fork in the road, take it." Whichever one you take (except the first one) will bring you out, so don't worry, you will exit into Charlotte Harbor. Turn to the right along the shoreline back to the boat ramp.

Sunset at Ponce de Leon Park

After the short trip through the mangroves re-load your gear and head to the beach area. Bring some chairs, some crackers and cheese, some wine, and some friends.

This is one of the best places north of Key West to watch a sunset. In fact, the paddle we recommend here is an afternoon paddle through the mangrove tunnels, followed by some wine and cheese on the beach as the sun sets on the harbor. You will have the perfect ending to a perfect day in Paradise.

Third disclaimer: There is no alcohol allowed in the public parks. Despite that disclaimer we stand by the above paragraph.

Directions to Ponce Park

From downtown Punta Gorda take E. Marion St out of downtown. Continue past Fisherman's Village on your right and continue for several miles. You will pass the Isles Yacht Club on your right then cross over two canal bridges. Continue on and you will see the sign for Ponce de Leon Park on your left. About 10 minutes from downtown Punta Gorda.

For rentals, our favorite local outfitter is O-SEA-D Aquatic Adventures, ask for Vince. You can reach them at:

http://www.oseadkayaking.com or phone 941-347-8102

Ponce de Leon Park

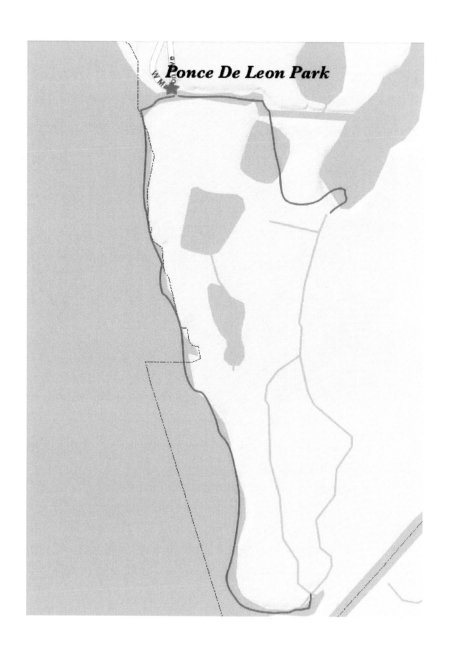

Chapter 16

Rock Springs Run

GPS address   5722 Baptist Camp Rd   Apopka

Tranquility along the river

This is a great 8 mile paddle downstream with all the "Old Florida" charm including the possibility of seeing deer, otters, and bear, as well as the varied and abundant Florida birds. It is rated as one of the best paddles in central Florida and it is highly recommended by us. The water is clear and teeming with fish. The flora is amazing and in the spring, when the wildflowers are in bloom, the sights, sounds and smells will blow you away.

After launching, paddle out a small canal and into the river. You will see a wide river that is shrunken down on both sides by

61

lily pads and water plants. In many spots the trees form a canopy overhead and for miles it is as pristine as you will find. There are several spots along the run where you can stop and relax, or get out and swim. Don't forget your camera! This is one paddle you'll want to remember. There are some tight turns along the way which will help improve your paddle skills but nothing that should challenge anyone who isn't a first time paddler.

At the bottom you can turn to the right if you want to see the spring head of the Wekiva River at Wekiva Springs State Park (about .7 mile).

Turning left will take you past the Wekiva Island Resort. Turn right at the Resort and directly past the resort is your take out and shuttle pick up spot. If you arrive early there are facilities at the resort you can use while waiting; including a tiki bar. After all, it was a long paddle and you don't want to get dehydrated.

Heron at Rock Springs Run

You can also do this paddle from Wekiva Island Resort (see Chapter 24) and go upstream and then return down without having to shuttle. Since the current is 3-4 mph this would be more difficult for novice paddlers. If you go that route just turn left after launching at the resort and at about .5 miles there is a small sign on the right for Rock Springs Run. Just head upstream until tired and float back down.

Both the Wekiva River and Rock Springs Run can be busy on weekends and holidays so we recommend a weekday trip. You can do this as an overnight and include the paddles in Ch 4 (Dora Canal) and Ch 18 (Silver River) on the same trip.

Directions to Kings Landing

Take I-75 North towards Tampa and take exit 261 onto I-4 East towards Orlando. Take exit 60 to Florida 429 North to Apopka. After about 30 miles take Florida 451. Follow 451 for several miles and take U.S. 441/Orange Blossom Trail towards Apopka. After 2.5 miles turn right onto U.S. 441/Florida 500 S/W Orange Blossom Trail and follow about 1.5 miles. Turn left onto County Road 435/S Park Ave for about 6 miles and turn right onto E Kelly Park Road. In less than 1/2 mile turn left onto Baptist Camp Road. Kings Landing Loomis Outfitters will be on right. Allow approximately 3 hours from Punta Gorda.

Kings Landing is the best place to launch if you want to paddle down the run and be shuttled back with your canoe/kayak (http://www.kingslandingfl.com). Call for hours 407-886-0859. The average trip takes 3-4 hours or a leisurely

4.5 hours. The pick up is at 4pm on weekdays so you should start by 11am. There is a $10 launch fee and a $10 shuttle fee. There are also rentals available for $30-50 depending on whether it's a 1 or 2 person craft. Rental fee includes the shuttle pick up. There is also a store here with snacks and supplies as well as restroom facilities.

Rock Springs Run/Wekiva River

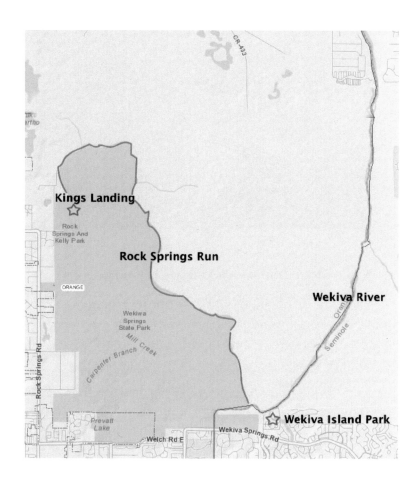

Chapter 17

Shell Creek

GPS address 35461 Washington Loop Rd.   Punta Gorda

Basking turtles along Shell Creek

When you try this paddle you will be hooked forever.

Shell Creek is one of our favorite local paddles. We have paddled it many times when we want to do a relaxing and scenic paddle close to home and it is also where we take guests from out of town.

This is another "Old Florida" paddle and is great for novice paddlers. It combines beautiful scenery and wildlife with an easy relaxed pace that guarantees to hook the first time paddler into wanting more. It is very undeveloped and you will

65

find it hard to believe you are still in civilization. There are less than a half dozen houses for the first couple of miles and after that nothing but wilderness.

As you make your way up the almost non-existent current the creek narrows and becomes more shallow. Palm trees hang over the creek. Sunlight peeks through the canopy highlighting the Morning Glories and making the flora come alive with nuanced color. Turtles are basking on the dead falls, and wildlife is abundant, including hawks, osprey and an occasional alligator.

Night heron at Shell Creek

It is an up and back paddle which can be done leisurely in 2-3 hours. You will eventually run out of water but can paddle about 5 miles before you do.

Directions to Hathaway Park

From I-75 exit 164 (or from downtown Punta Gorda) take RT 17 North towards Arcadia. Drive several miles until you see the "Royal Thai" restaurant on the right. Immediately past the restaurant take a right onto Washington Loop Road. Drive approximately 4 miles and look for the entrance to Hathaway Park on your left. You can take this entrance and launch from the boat ramp where there is a parking fee or you can continue on to the second entrance and launch from the kayak launch with limited free parking. Allow approximately 20 minutes from Punta Gorda.

Whichever launch you choose unload your gear close by and park in the parking area.

The park has a port-a-potty for a restroom at the kayak launch entrance but a regular restroom at the boat launch entrance. There are picnic facilities at both. There are no rentals available on-site but we have a great outfitter who will service you there. Call O-SEA-D Aquatic Adventures in Punta Gorda (they are one of the best outfitters we know) and ask for Vince. You can reach them at: http://www.oseadkayaking.com or phone 941-347-8102

If you put in from the canoe launch turn to the right out of the small pond you are in, then turn right to go up the creek; did you bring your paddle?

If you launch from the boat ramp you are already in the creek. Just head to the right.

Shell Creek

Chapter 18

Silver River

GPS address   9560 NE 28th Lane   Silver Springs

Wild Rhesus monkey

The wildlife you can see on this paddle is amazing and includes alligators, fish, turtles, wood ducks, otters, anhingas, ibis, herons and monkeys. Yes, monkeys! You will find yourself pulling off into small eddies to get out of the current to watch the monkeys playing along the shore or even jumping into the water from the trees.

The monkeys were imported to the area by a local tour operator, one Colonel Tooey, in the late 1930's. They were put on a small island he had built and he assumed they would be isolated there to be an attraction for his river boat tours.

Little did he know that Rhesus Monkeys are excellent swimmers and they instantly departed his little island for greener pastures....all along the river. He was right though, they are indeed an attraction. Note: *Do not* feed the monkeys! These are wild Rhesus monkeys who can become aggressive if they think you have food to offer. The only thing that could spoil a trip this beautiful is a visit to the hospital for a monkey bite.

The river is a translucent blue, fairly narrow and very scenic. The paddle is through protected park land and has virtually no development. Although you will see an occasional motor boat along the way they are reduced to a no wake speed.

Wood ducks along the Silver River

Once you are on the Silver River the first thing you will notice is the current. It runs about 3 mph against you and is somewhat challenging. This is not a very difficult paddle but it does require some stamina. You have to paddle but it is well worth the effort. If you stop you will be losing ground.

It is 5 miles upriver to the spring head at Silver Springs Nature Park. There is a State Park with a canoe/kayak launch about 3.5 miles up and it is a good spot to stop, get out for a break and have some lunch, a snack, or use the port-a-potty.

The return trip is the reward for the paddle up. You'll enjoy a slow leisurely float downstream while enjoying all the spectacular scenery along the way.

The entire trip takes about 4 hours and you will go home tired but with some of the best pictures you have ever taken.

Directions to Ray Wayside Park

Drive I-75 North to exit 352. Merge onto SR 40 E towards Ocala/Silver Springs. Drive approximately 12 miles and bear right onto NE 28th Lane. Ray Wayside Park will be on your right. Allow approximately 3 hours from Punta Gorda.

When you arrive at Ray Wayside Park get an envelope at the entrance and use the drop box. There is a $3 fee. Make sure you put your receipt on your dashboard.

Drive straight past the restrooms, past the boat ramp all the way to the back left corner. There is a canoe/kayak launch a very short walk from the parking area. Unload your gear and then park in the lot (don't park in the boat trailer section).

After launching, head out of the small basin and at the end of the short canal turn *right*. Take note of the canal location for the return trip. If you turn to the left you will be joining the Ocklawaha River and that is another paddle, for another day, in the next edition.

Ray Wayside Park has restroom facilities and a picnic area. For rentals contact:

http://www.paddle-dog.com or phone 352-625-2719

For other paddles in the area see Dora Canal (Ch 4) Wekiva River (Ch 24) and Rock Springs Run (Ch 16).

Silver River

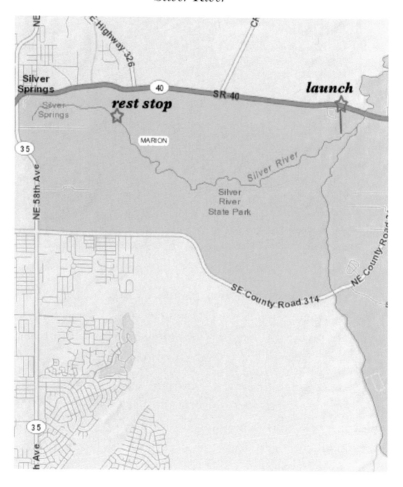

Chapter 19

Telegraph Creek

GPS address   1660 S Franklin Lock Road   Alva

Barred owl at Telegraph Creek

This paddle is a hidden gem right off the busy waters of the Caloosahatchee River. Although you are never far from civilization you feel like you are going further and further into the wilderness with every stroke of your paddle.

As you enter the creek there are several homes along the shores. One of the first ones on the left is home to a flock of wild peacocks and depending on the time of day you may be serenaded by their calls. It eventually narrows down and becomes more remote.

You will pass several farms along the right side where you will see horses, but the highlight is the alpaca farm. All along the banks are wild ducks, turtles, alpacas and if you thought that was a camel you saw...it was. Past the alpaca farm the water becomes narrower and more remote and beautiful. You are now basking in the silence and beauty of the creek while seeing herons, geese, ducks, turtles, wildflowers and owls. As you get deeper into the creek the flora and fauna become even more impressive.

Paddle on to your heart's content and when ready turn around and head back. Most of our trips with the group we lead last about 2 hours (an hour out and an hour back) followed by a group picnic lunch, but this is one of those paddles that makes you want to skip lunch and go on all day.

Pretty cannot describe it...Peaceful is an understatement. As the television cereal ad says…."Try it…You'll like it!"

Baby alpacas playing along the creek

Directions to Franklin Lock South

From I-75 South take exit 141 (just over the Caloosahatchee Bridge) and take a left off the exit (SR 80 East). Drive approximately 6.8 miles and turn left onto Pine Ave. At the end of Pine Ave turn right onto Old Olga Road and the WP Franklin Lock entrance will be on your left. Follow the road into the park and drive to the boat ramp. Allow approximately 45 minutes drive time from Punta Gorda.

You are now on the Caloosahatchee River at the Franklin Lock, south side. The park has bathroom facilities, a swimming beach, and plenty of picnic areas but no rentals available on site.

You can unload your gear at the ramp and park your vehicle in the main lot for free. (the boat launch area is for boat trailers only and there is a fee). There is a grassy area right next to the boat ramp where you can launch. According to the Park Ranger we spoke to you can launch anywhere in the park but not on the beach area.

After putting in turn left and paddle past the lock. Paddle across the Caloosahatchee (this is a short open water paddle of 10-15 minutes) to the other side and continue heading to the left. In another 10 minutes of paddling along the shore line you will come to the entrance to Telegraph Creek. Just before the red channel marker there is a sharp right turn and the property at the inlet has a white stone/coral bank facing you.

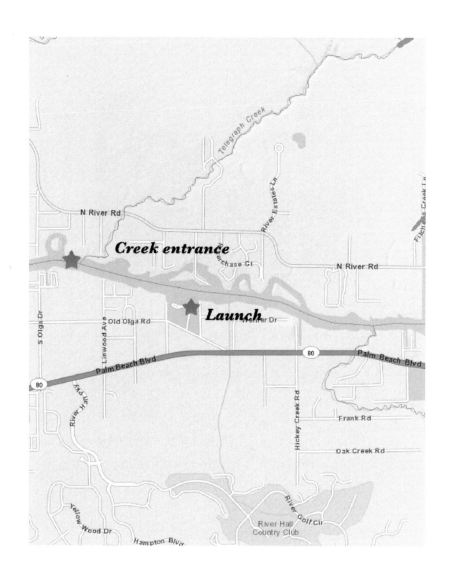

Chapter 20

Turtle Beach / Siesta Key

GPS address 8797 Blind Pass Rd.   Sarasota

Great blue heron

For those who want to get out of the closed in mangrove tunnels and cypress swamps once in a while this is a short but pretty paddle around the marine preserve island in Sarasota Bay.

It is a very relaxed and easy paddle where you are likely to see dolphin, birds, NO alligators for those of you who are wary (this is all salt water, thus, no gators) and manatees. We even encountered a group of mating manatees once....we had no idea they could move that fast!

This is a great paddle for a hot summer day when you just want to get outside but it's too hot for anything else. There is a great little beach area after you come around the island and are heading back. You can stop here and walk over the dune and take a dip in the Gulf if you'd like.

When you're finished paddling go right across the street to Turtle Beach and spend the rest of the day relaxing on the Gulf of Mexico.

After you launch at the park area head out of the channel into the bay. You will see the island right in front of you. Turn left and paddle around the island in a loop.

Take your time and enjoy the warm water, the salt air and the numerous birds along the way.

Taking a break and a quick swim on Siesta Key

Directions to Blind Pass Rd boat launch

Take I-75 North to exit 205. Turn left onto FL-72 W/ Clark Road. Clark Road turns into Stickney Point Road. At end of Stickney Point Road turn left onto Midnight Pass Road. Travel 2.6 miles and turn right onto Turtle Beach Road. Take left onto Blind Pass Road where parking lot and boat ramp area are on your left. Allow approximately 1 hour from Punta Gorda.

There are several picnic tables at the launch and restroom facilities a short walk from there.

Rentals are available here but are expensive. The outfitters in this area will only do full day rentals, even if you are only going for a few hours.

You can reach them at:

http://www.adventurekayakoutfitters.com or phone 941-779-7426

Turtle Beach

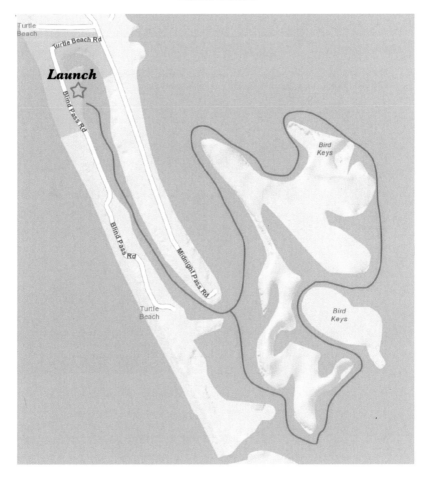

Chapter 21

Venice Myakka River Park

GPS address   7501 Laurel Rd East   *Nokomis*

Solitude...Solitude...Solitude

When it comes to pristine Florida wilderness you can't do much better than this.

This is a serene and remote paddle through protected and undeveloped land. The shores are lined with live oak trees, cabbage palms, and pine trees. If you go in the spring you will see many wildflowers, such as Leavenworth's tickseed (Florida's State Wildflower), black eyed susans, and purple passionflower.

Wildlife will include alligators as well as the usual array of tropical birds, turtles and fish.

The river starts out several hundred feet across and slowly narrows down as you progress. There is very little current and it is a very easy and relaxing paddle. You can go upstream as far as you'd like and then turn back. We did a very easy 6 miles in a little over 3 hours.

There is a narrow and shallow area about 2.5 miles upstream called Rocky Ford where the bottom changes to hard, rock-like, limestone and marl stone.

In dry season some parts of the river above Rocky Ford, up to and beyond the Lower Myakka Lake, become dry and impassable but this particular paddle is a must all year round.

Myakka River

The entire Myakka River covers 68 miles and flows from the Hardee/Manatee County line all the way to Charlotte Harbor. A 34 mile portion of the Myakka River in Sarasota County, which includes this paddle, was designated as a *"Wild and Scenic River"* in 1985 by the Florida Legislature.

Directions to Venice Myakka River Park

Take I-75 North to exit 195. Turn right off exit onto Laurel Road. Follow Laurel Road a couple of miles to the end. The park is at the end of the road on your left. Allow about 40 minutes from Punta Gorda.

This is a small park and you can only drive in as far as the walkway. You can unload and park right by the stanchions and it is about a 75 yard walk to the launch. It is a floating dock launch so this is a good time to practice your dock launch skills; and bring your wheels.

After you launch, paddle to the right until you come to the main river, then turn left. You are now heading upstream towards Myakka River State Park.

There are no rentals available on site but there are several picnic areas and restroom facilities. Some information about the park can be found at:

http://www.venicegov.com/Park_links/venice_myakka

Venice Myakka trail

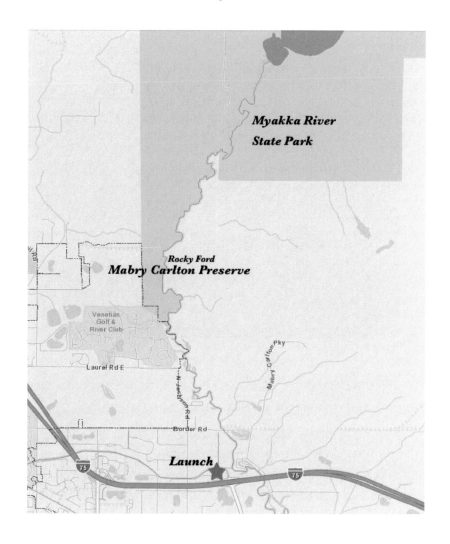

Chapter 22

Weedon Island

GPS address 1800 Weedon Drive N.E.   St Petersburg

About to enter the mangrove trail

Weedon Island Preserve has a great little trail that takes you through and around the preserve nestled in Tampa Bay.

It is a numbered trail that will bring you through canopied mangrove tunnels and around several small islands. The marked trail is 4 miles long and will take about 3 hours. The last mile is out of the mangroves in shallow open water.

After launching, head across the bay to the marked trail. If it is a windy day you may have to work a little harder getting back but it has never been a problem for even our novice paddlers.

This is shallow tidal area so you must check the tides before you go. You will not be able to get through the mangroves at low tide; mid to high tide is best.

When we do this paddle we stay overnight in Tarpon Springs, a quaint Greek sponge diving village with lots of shops and restaurants and some of the best Greek food around.

If you don't like Greek food there are plenty of other options as well and if you've never been to Tarpon Springs it should be on your list...especially if you need a new sponge.

This is a great paddle to do in conjunction with an overnight trip to Weeki Wachee Springs (see chapter 23).

Negotiating the canopied mangrove tunnels at Weedon Island Preserve

Fourth Disclaimer: When we talk about overnight paddle trips we do NOT mean camping out. We are retired, remember? We find a couple of great paddles in the area of a neat little Florida town; a decent hotel nearby, with a pool and a bar…..and *VOILA*! An overnight paddle for *recreational* paddlers.

Directions to Weedon Island Preserve

Take I-75 North to exit 228 to I-275 North. Follow I-275 North over Sunshine Skyway and take exit 26A. Merge eastbound on 54th Ave North for 1.8 miles. Turn left onto 4th St North (Rte 687). After approx. 1.8 miles turn right onto 83rd Ave (Patica Road). Continue on to San Martin Blvd for approx. ½ mile then turn right onto Ridgeway Drive NE, then right again onto Weedon Drive NE. Follow Weedon Drive NE to the end to the fishing pier and kayak launch. Allow approximately 1 hour and forty-five minutes from Punta Gorda.

When you arrive at the launch unload your gear and try to get one of the few nearby parking spots. If you don't, there is a larger parking area back up the road and you'll have a good walk back to the launch. There are restrooms right at the launch but not a lot of parking.

Rentals are available at http://www.sweetwaterkayaks.com

Rates are $17 per hour and $40 a half day.

Weedon Island

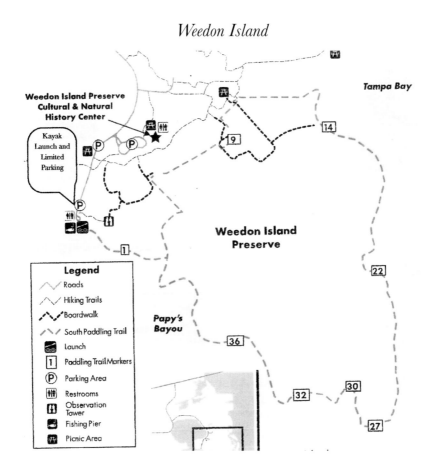

Chapter 23

Weeki Wachee Springs

GPS address 6131 Commercial Way   Spring Hill

The crystal clear water of Weeki Wachee Springs

This is a beautiful and relaxing 5.5 mile trip down river with crystal clear water, overhanging natural canopy, birds, turtles, manatees, and otter. This has to be one of the most scenic paddles you'll ever take, especially since it's all downstream and you will be shuttled back to the park.

You'll have lots of time to watch for wildlife and enjoy the cypress, oaks and palm trees as the sunlight filters through them into the blue green spring waters. The first time paddlers on this trip are always awed by its beauty, as are we, who have done it multiple times.

Your paddle/float trip will take about 3 hours. There are many twists and turns to navigate but the current is not that strong; just paddle through the turns and keep your nose headed downstream. There are several spots along the river where you can stop on a sandy area and get out, stretch, have a snack or just wade in the clearest water you've ever seen.

This is an easy paddle and many first timers have done it without any problem. The current is slower at the end and you will find yourself having to do a little more paddling the last mile. Bear to the left and watch for signs for Rogers Park (if you get to the bridge you have just passed it). The outfitter staff will be there to assist you and your canoe/kayak while you wait for the pickup shuttle. The last shuttle is at 5pm so be sure to time your trip accordingly.

Serenity now

Do this paddle as an overnight and take in Weedon Island (see chapter 22) on the way up, stay in Tarpon Springs overnight and paddle the springs in the morning.

Directions to Weeki Wachee Springs State Park

Take I-75 North to exit 278 and merge onto I-275 North. Drive approximately 30 miles and take exit 30 to Florida 686 (W. Roosevelt Blvd). Follow signs for County Road 296 West and merge onto 118th Ave. Follow signs for and take U.S. 19 North for approximately 48 miles. Weeki Wachee Springs will be on left. Enter parking area and go to rear left corner of parking area to enter the canoe/kayak launch area. Allow approximately 2.5 hours from Punta Gorda.

After entering the launch area, unload as close as possible to the main building. All rentals and launch fees are handled there; there are bathroom facilities, a small store and then there is a short walk beyond that to the actual launch area.

Don't make the walk any longer than you have to. If you have wheels bring them.

If you are renting you will pick up your rental at the launch. There is a launch fee of $5 per canoe/kayak and a $10 fee for the return shuttle for you and your canoe/kayak back to the parking lot. Rentals are available for $30 which includes the return shuttle.

Weekends may be very busy so call them for reservations. phone 352-597-8484. For Additional information go to:

http://www.paddlingadventures.com.

Weeki Wachee Springs

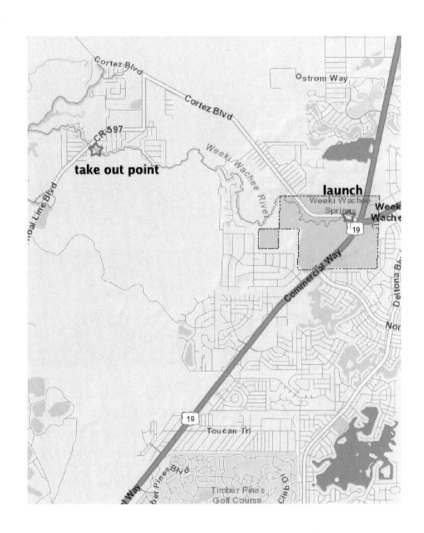

Chapter 24

Wekiva River

GPS address   1014 Miami Springs Dr.   Longwood

Paradise here I come

This is another relaxing, remote, and scenic paddle that should be done very leisurely. You don't want to miss the abundant aquatic plants and flowers as well as the wildlife all around you; such as otters, ibis, limpkins, alligators, deer, great herons, osprey and even bald eagles.

Mother Nature put it here...the State of Florida protects it....it's up to *us* to enjoy it!

After you launch, paddle out to the right and follow the river downstream as far as you'd like before heading back.

There is a very slight current on the return trip, nothing difficult, but if you tire easily consider that you have to paddle back.

You can go about 20 miles on this section. We usually head out for about an hour or two before turning, leaving some energy on the return trip to paddle past the launch area and on to the spring head which is less than 1 mile further upstream. This is also the same launch to use if you want to paddle Rock Springs Run (Ch 16) upstream.

If you do decide to travel further downstream there is a park about 8.5 miles from your launch site which has a canoe/ kayak launch and bathroom facilities (Wilson's Landing) and another about 10 miles (Katie's Landing) with a port-a-potty. If you decide to paddle the entire 20 miles you will make it to High Banks Landing which also has a portable toilet facility.

Wekiva River near Wekiva Springs Park

Directions to Wekiva Island Resort

Take I-75 North to exit 261 and follow I-4 East until exit 94. Turn left and follow 434 West approximately 1 mile then turn right onto Wekiva Springs Road. After about 3 miles turn right onto Miami Springs Drive follow to end and turn right and enter resort. Allow approximately 3 hours from Punta Gorda.

Enter the park and head to the boat ramp and unload your gear then park anywhere in the parking area.

There is a $6 per canoe/kayak launch fee and there are also rentals available for $30 for entire day. There is no need to make a rental reservation as they have plenty of kayaks. You pay at the tiki bar across the lot near the water.

The park has bathroom facilities, food, drinks, and activities. It can be very crowded on weekends so go during the week for a more relaxed atmosphere.

For more park information go to:

http://www.wekivaisland.com.

For other paddles in the area see Dora Canal (Ch 4) Silver River (Ch 18) and Rock Springs Run (Ch 16).

Wekiva River

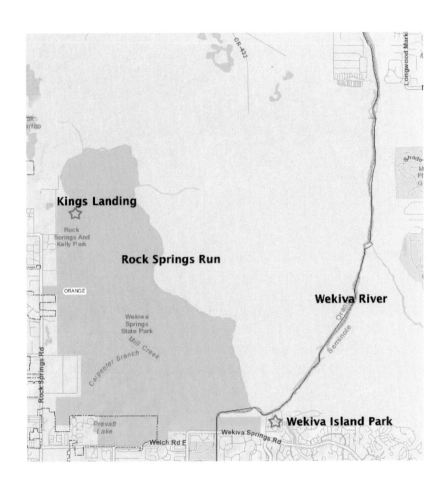

Chapter 25

Woolverton Trail

GPS address   12575 Placida Rd   *Placida*

White pelicans

This is a wonderfully maintained and numbered trail that meanders in and out of overhanging mangrove tunnels which teem with wild birds and stunning natural beauty. Along the way to the trail it is not uncommon to see manatee or a dolphin.

Once inside the trail it is serene and beautiful, and you forget that you are still in the middle of civilization along the Intracoastal Waterway. There are several openings in the tunnels that bring you out of the trail into open water, so if you find yourself in open water too soon just head back in and follow the numbers (keep referencing the map the outfitter gave you). Several hours will go by without your even noticing.

Our launch point is from Grande Tours, an outfitter that has it all. They offer rentals, canoe, kayak and paddle board sales, sunset cruises, fishing, and guided eco tours. They are extremely friendly and helpful every time we go there and it is always our pleasure to do business with them. No, this is NOT a paid advertisement. We just like them.

There is a $6 launch fee if you bring your own canoe/kayak (which includes a map of the area and the trail) or you can rent one for $27.50 for 2 hours, up to $47.50 for all day. Parking is free and there is a small picnic area and restroom facilities.

In the mangrove tunnels on Woolverton Trail

Directions to Grande Tours Kayak and Paddle Board Center

From Punta Gorda take U.S. 41 North and turn left onto SR 776. Follow SR 776 and turn left onto SR 771 (Gasparilla Rd; it becomes SR 775 in Placida) until you come to Grande Tours on the right at the intersection of SR 775 and the Boca Grande Causeway. Allow approximately 45 minutes from Punta Gorda.

Pull your vehicle up to the carpeted launch area and unload before parking in the lot.

After you launch, use the map they give you and head to the right and follow the map to the entrance of the Woolverton Trail.

You can contact Grande Tours at:

http://www.grandetours.com.

Woolverton Trail

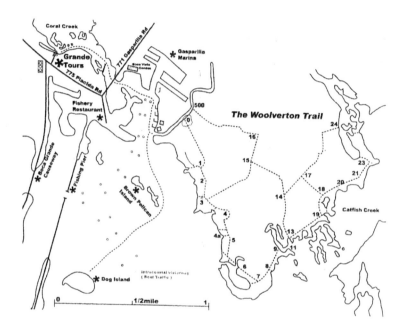

Afterward

So, now that you have read this book, tried the paddles, and discovered that we have missed some really great waters, don't worry; we are taking time to smell the roses....we'll get to them all, eventually!

Keep your eye out for our next edition:

"More Paddles in Paradise."

You can reach us at paddlesinparadise@gmail.com, or visit our website: http://www.paddlesinparadise.com.

About the Authors

Past

Ed Higgins spent 32 years as a firefighter for the City of Lynn, Massachusetts, retiring in 2008 as the Chief of the Department. He was an avid fisherman and canoeist when he wasn't working, and was an instructor in the Aquatic Resources Program for the State of Massachusetts. As a private pilot with his own plane he and Deb spent many hours in the skies over Massachusetts, New Hampshire, Maine and Vermont searching for paradise. They found it in Florida.

Deb Higgins was a Certified Microsoft Engineer and performed various jobs within the City of Lynn Comptroller's Office and the Lynn Fire Department; computerizing the Fire Department payroll as well as its accounting and record keeping systems. Deb also was an Assistant Treasurer and Loan Officer for the Firefighter's Credit Union and the Financial Manager of the condo association where they lived.

Present

Ed & Deb are now retired and living in Punta Gorda, Florida. They are the leaders of a kayak group within the Punta Gorda Boat Club and spend most of their time playing, relaxing, boating, traveling and paddling. Ok,....*sometimes* they hydrate by the pool.

They love to go exploring; especially to find new places where they can get lost in the solitude and beauty of nature. They love even more bringing others to these places and introducing them to "Paradise."